KINDLE PAPERWHITE USER GUIDE

THE Utimate Guide To Help You Unleashed And Master Your Kindle Device

By

Kelvin L. Wilson

Copyright © 2020 Kelvin L. Wilson

All rights reserved. No part of this book shall be reproduced, stored in a retrieval system, or transmitted by any means, electronic, mechanical, photocopying, recording, or otherwise, without written permission from the publisher. Although every precaution has been taken in the preparation of this book, the publisher and author assume no responsibility for errors or omissions. Nor is any liability assumed for damages resulting from the use of the information contained herein.

Table of Contents

INTRODUCTION 1

AMAZON KINDLE PAPERWHITE REVIEW: THE NEW STANDARD 1

STANDARDS 3

WATERPROOF 3

CHAPTER ONE 5

HOW TO SETUP YOUR KINDLE PAPERWHITE 5

HOW DO I SET UP KINDLE PAPERWHITE 6

TOOLBAR 7

STATUS INDICATOR 7

CONNECTIVITY 7

THE BOTTOM LINE.. 8

CHAPTER TWO 9

HOW TO TURN OFF KINDLE "SPECIAL OFFERS......9

CHAPTER THREE 12

HOW TO NAVIGATE YOUR KINDLE: 12

TO VIEW ALL BOOKS IN YOUR LIBRARY, CLICK MY LIBRARY ON THE HOME PAGE. 12

CHAPTER FOUR..13

THE TOUCH SCREEN ON YOUR KINDLE PAPERWHITE..13

WHAT HAPPENED TO THE START BUTTON?.........13

TOUCH, SWIPE AND PINCH 13

TOUCH 14

SWIPE 14

LONG TOUCH OR PINCH 15

CUT AND TRIMMED 16

TOUCHSCREEN ZONES 16

Top zone 18

Central Zone 18

Left area 18

CHAPTER FIVE 19

REMOVE TITLES FROM YOUR SENTENCES 19

CHAPTER SIX 20

HOW TO DELETE BOOKS FROM YOUR KINDLE ... 20

HOW TO DELETE A BOOK FROM THE KINDLE
LIBRARY 20

WHAT ABOUT BOOKS FROM THE KINDLE LOAN
LIBRARY? 21

CHAPTER SEVEN 23

DOWNLOAD COLLECTIONS TO YOUR KINDLE E-
READER 23

SELECT FILTER AND THEN COLLECTIONS 23

TO DELETE ITEMS FROM A COLLECTION OR TO
DELETE A COLLECTION 24

CHAPTER EIGHT 25

CHILD PROFILE ON YOUR KINDLE E-READER 25

CHAPTER NINE.. 26

   ZOOM IN ON IMAGES... 26

CHAPTER TEN...27

   INTERACT WITH YOUR DOCUMENTS 27

   TO CHANGE YOUR DEFAULT DICTIONARY: 27

   SEARCH... 28

   BOOKMARKS 29

   FOOTNOTES 30

   BEFORE YOU GO. 30

CHAPTER ELEVEN 33

   HOW TO LOOK IN A BOOK ON YOUR KINDLE FIRE
....33

CHAPTER TWELVE...35

   VOCABULARY BUILDER...35

   TRUN OFF VOCABULARY BUILDER 36

CHAPTER THIRTEEN 37

   KINDLE FREETIME..37

   SET UP THE KINDLE FREETIME..............................37

   KINDLE FREETIME.. 38

CHAPTER FOURTEEN 40

   GOODREADS ON THE KINDLE................................ 40

   Updates 41

   My Shelves 41

Friends: 41

HOW TO SHARE HIGHLIGHTS AND NOTES ON KINDLE PAPERWHITE WITH GOODREADS 42

CHAPTER FIVETEEN 46

HOW TO USE THE KINDLE PAPERWHITE BROWSE 46

HOW TO CONNECT TO THE INTERNET 48

CHAPTER SIXTEEN 49

SCREENSHOT 49

CHAPTER SEVENTEEN 50

HOW TO USE THE KINDLE MATCHBOOK 50

CHAPTER EIGHTEEN 52

HOW TO BORROW BOOKS ON KINDLE PAPERWHITE 52

CHAPTER NINETEEN 55

HOW TO READ EPUB ON KINDLE PAPERWHITE ..55

CONVERT EPUB TO KINDLE FORMAT (3 WAYS) ...56

TOOL 1: CONVERT EPUB TO CALIBER 56

TOOL 2: CONVERT EPUB TO ACTIVATION WITH ONLINE CONVERTER 57

Epubor 58

Zamzar 58

CloudConvert 58

CHAPTER TWENTY 59

KINDLE DICTIONARY GUIDE:................................59

HOW TO ADD, EDIT, AND CREATE PERSONALIZED KINDLE DICTIONARIES 59

HOW TO CHANGE THE DEFAULT KINDLE DICTIONARY 60

HOW TO CREATE CUSTOM KINDLE DICTIONARIES 61

CHAPTER TWENTY ONE.......................................63

CUSTOMIZE YOUR TEXT DISPLAY 63

COMIC AND MANGA BOOK.....................................63

CHILDREN'S BOOKS 63

CHAPTER TWENTY TWO 65

MANAGE YOUR KINDLE LIBRARY..........................65

WITH COLLECTIONS 66

TO CREATE A NEW COLLECTION:.......................... 66

TIPS ON CLOUD COLLECTIONS: 67

INTRODUCTION

AMAZON KINDLE PAPERWHITE REVIEW: THE NEW STANDARD

The 2018 Amazon Kindle Paperwhite is a sophisticated, easy-to-use e-reader, now water and 4G resistant. Photo: Samuel Gibbs / The Guardian

The new Amazon Kindle Paperwhite is thinner, lighter and now water resistant, which sets a new standard for what an e-reader should be.

Only so far can you print a single click. Technically, the Kindle Paperwhite is more than just an e-reader, as it now has Bluetooth for audio book playback. But it is still a book reader, simple and easy.

All a book reader needs is a beautiful, clear and legible screen. Paperwhite has it - a 6in 300ppi e-ink display that is clear and legible in all conditions, complete with good, uniform light when needed.

Compared to the 2015 Paperwhite, the design has been further simplified. It is another black rectangle with an e-ink screen in the middle. This time, the screen is flat with the body, a seamless front end that was previously committed to the more expensive Voyage and Oasis.

Amazon Kindle Paperwhite Review

The screen is now flat with the body to fit and lock over the front of the white paper. Photo: Samuel Gibbs / The Guardian

The body is 0.9 mm thinner, 1 mm smaller and 2 mm narrower than the old white paper, but it is not really noticeable if you do not compare them side by side. The edges look almost the same, the soft touch plastic body feels the same, there is the same button and the micro-USB port on the bottom and the same LED that lights up when charging.

What is impressive is the weight reduction of 23g, which brings the 2018 white paper to 182g. brighter is better when it comes to reading. Dual storage at 8 GB on the cheapest model is also welcome, especially if you want to load an audio book.

STANDARDS

- Display: 6in E-Paper (300ppi)
- Weight: 182g (4G version 191g)
- Connectivity: Wi-Fi (optional 3G), Bluetooth

WATERPROOF

The LED on the button lights up when you turn off the electronic reader and indicates the charging status when it is on. Photo: Samuel Gibbs / The Guardian

This year, the water resistance is 2 meters to 60 minutes, which means that trips to the beach or pool are less risky. It is worth noting that white paper does not float, so it may be best not to take it out to sea, but a quick dip or a dip will be fine.

Battery life: rated for reading for about 21 hours

How far you are in a book depends on how fast you read, but I have found it convenient to extend a book of 400 pages between screen charges at half brightness or more. Turn on wifi and 4G if you have them and the battery life will be significantly reduced. It goes into deep sleep if you do not use it for a long time, which helps maintain battery life even with the ability to connect.

 The X-ray image is even better for tracking characters and other bits. Photo: Samuel Gibbs / The Guardian

The reading experience is the same as any recent Kindle touch screen. Drag or drop to edit pages, tap at the top to enter the menu, including quick settings such as flight mode, brightness control, and page options.

Switching is a bit easier now, as there are no screen edges, but the side-scroll buttons are better for manual reading - you still need 110 110 for the Kindle Oasis for those who spend on an Amazon e-reader.

There are many fonts, text sizes, spaces and paragraph alignments to choose from, as well as the Amazon X-ray service that helps you keep track of characters, locations and other tracks.

If you have both the audiobook and the e-book, you can sync between the two and choose either the format you prefer, which works surprisingly well.

CHAPTER ONE

HOW TO SETUP YOUR KINDLE PAPERWHITE

The Kindle Paperwhite is the latest version of the e-book reader introduced by Amazon Inc. Setting up the Kindle Paperwhite is important for using Kindle services. The device comes with a 6-inch 212 PPI screen and multi-touch enabled. Kindle Paperwhite comes with a built-in light for better resolution. If you have the kindle paperwhite Good! you are about to enjoy a perfect reading online experience. The Kindle Paperwhite comes with all the fascinating features that an e-reader would love. So if you don't know how to use Kindle Paperwhite, read on and find out everything you need to know about the device for setup.

HOW DO I SET UP KINDLE PAPERWHITE

On turning on your Kindle Paperwhite, the first screen will tells you about the built-in screen light, high resolution, and battery life.

Here, you need to select the language in which you want to use your Kindle Paperwhite. The default language is English. n change it any time. To go to settings, you can click on the menu icon on your home screen.

The Kindle Paperwhite supports a touch screen interface that allows users to select options with a simple touch. For the other task, users need to tilt their finger across the screen, it is very useful when the user wants to turn the page while reading the Kindle e-book.

The device also supports the on-screen keyboard that can be used to type input. The keyboard is very easy to use and works like a computer.

TOOLBAR

When you tap at the top of the Kindle screen, you will see the toolbar and the shortcut and buttons that can be of help in navigating your Kindle after setup. This includes the Home button, the Search button, the Menu button, and the other additional buttons.

The user can see the secondary toolbar when reading the book.

STATUS INDICATOR

On the Kindle Paperwhite home screen, the user can see the indicator that reports the status of the device. On the next screen, your Kindle Paperwhite will ask you to connect to Wi-Fi.

CONNECTIVITY

Connecting Kindle Paperwhite to Wi-Fi is a very simple process.

Tap the 'Menu' button on the home screen and go to 'Settings'.

In the settings menu you can see the option 'Wi-Fi Networks'.

Touch WiFi networks to see the list of available Wi-Fi networks. Connect to one.

Enter the password to connect to Wi-Fi.

When your device 3 is activated, it automatically connects to the 3G network by default. When you have completed the first steps to set up Kindle Paperwhite, you must register your device to use the service. Either your device is pre-registered or you must register it. If you purchased the Kindle Paperwhite with your Amazon account, you can pre-register it; otherwise, please register it with your Amazon login credentials.

THE BOTTOM LINE

I hope the steps above help you set up a Kindle Paperwhite device. So, complete the installation process and use Kindle services for the best online reading experience. In case you have any questions or problems, you can contact the experts and follow their advice to complete the setup.

CHAPTER TWO
HOW TO TURN OFF KINDLE
"SPECIAL OFFERS"

If you purchased a Kindle Fire Tablet or e-book reader from Amazon, you may see ads and recommended books. In addition to the hard disk space, color, Wi-Fi / mobile options, there is also an option with special offers that is default. This is the option that displays ads and suggestions. If you click More, which is in a much smaller font and therefore easy to miss, you will see a pop-up window that explains not very clearly - what you see.

The good news is that you can also pay for it when you get the Kindle - even if it costs you 10 that you did not pay at the time of purchase.

To turn off ads and "special offers", go to the Amazon website, sign in, and then click to manage your content and devices, and then click on the devices above. You will see a list of your Kindles, as well as all Amazon Alexa devices, as well as any phones or tablets you have installed in the Kindle app.

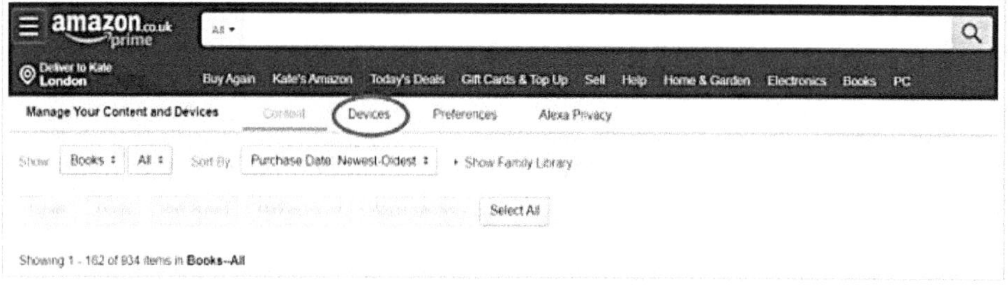

Tap the three-dot box in the left side of the Kindle from which you want to remove the ads, then click the down arrow next to Special Offers in the box that opens. Click Edit next to Record and follow the instructions

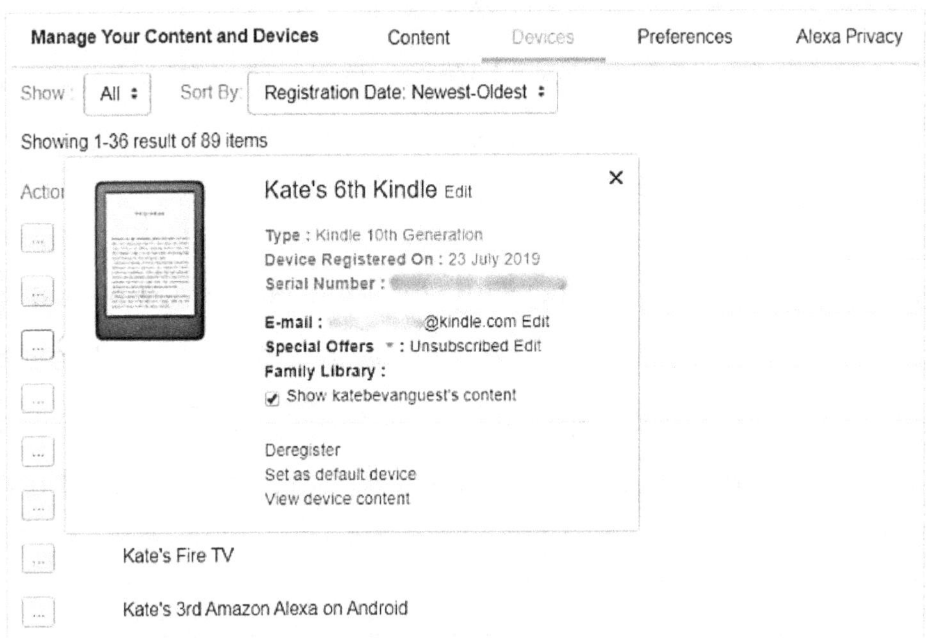

You will receive a one-time cancellation fee, which is usually £ 10.

When you're done, the next time you turn on the Kindle and connect to Wi-Fi, you'll not see the ads.

CHAPTER THREE

HOW TO NAVIGATE YOUR KINDLE

Tap the home (home icon) to return to the main page at any time. You can also press the arrow button to return anywhere.

Tap the gear icon to access all settings. There you will find My Account, Home & Family Library, Wireless, Device Options, Reading Options, Language & Dictionaries, Parental Controls and Legal We will look at many of these options later in this guide.

TO VIEW ALL BOOKS IN YOUR LIBRARY, CLICK MY LIBRARY ON THE HOME PAGE.

As you read, tap at the top of your screen and the menus will appear. Click Go to and you will see the contents of the book. You can go from chapter to chapter. You can also press notes to view your highlighted snippets.

CHAPTER FOUR

THE TOUCH SCREEN ON YOUR KINDLE PAPERWHITE

If you are an experienced Kindle Touch owner, you should know the following information. However, if you are upgrading from a button with Kindle or are new in general, then the following basic guide can get you started.

WHAT HAPPENED TO THE START BUTTON

Each Kindle Pre-Paperwhite has a physical home button that brings the device back to the home screen with just a press

If you are reading a book or other content and do not see the toolbar, simply click on the top of the screen to upload it.

TOUCH, SWIPE AND PINCH

All the usual uses of the Kindle Paperwhite - open books, turn pages, bookmark, etc involve some simple touchscreen gestures, such as touching and swiping. (We notice some cases where the behavior is a little different than what you might expect.)

Unlike Amazon's previous touchscreen device, the Kindle Paperwhite has a capacitive touchscreen, which means it only responds to an unlucky finger or stylus that mimics the touch of a finger.

TOUCH

A simple touch is the most common gesture you can use with Kindle Paperwhite. Do you see a screen button and want to activate it? Touch the button. View the list of books on your device? Touch one to open it.

When reading a book or other content, touch the forward page (see next page), the back page (see previous page), or display a menu of commands. What happens when you write a page of a book depends on which part of the screen you are writing.

SWIPE

If you swipe or slide the finger from right to left horizontally or diagonally across the screen, it moves sideways. The way is similar to making a page of paper into a printed book. To scroll back, scroll from left to right.

If you read a book or other content, sweep or touch the page.

If you want a page forward or backward when viewing a book list on the Home screen, swipe, do not touch. Clicking on a book title (or other content) on the Home screen opens the article to read.

When swiping, you only need to move your finger a short distance. You can probably tilt (or touch) without moving your hands from your reading position.

LONG TOUCH OR PINCH

For a long touch, also called a long press, touch the screen for a few seconds before releasing it. In general, a long touch results in a special action, depending on what you are looking at at the time.

For example, when viewing a book page, you may touch a word for a while to show its definition. When you see a list of books on the home screen, a long touch on a particular book shows options such as adding the book and reading a collection and its description.

By pressing and holding the title of an e-book sample that appears on the Home screen, you can purchase the book, read the description, or delete the sample from your device.

CUT AND TRIMMED

When reading a book or other content, place two fingers (or one finger and one thumb) on the touchscreen and slide them together. This pinching motion reduces the size of the font. Spread your fingers apart, meaning without hooks, to increase the font size. You only need to move your finger a short distance to change the font size.

You can see a lag between the pinch and remove the movements and a change in the size of the text. Fingers move slowly helps.

TOUCHSCREEN ZONES

The Kindle Paperwhite display is configured with crown zones that are designed to make pages easy with one finger.

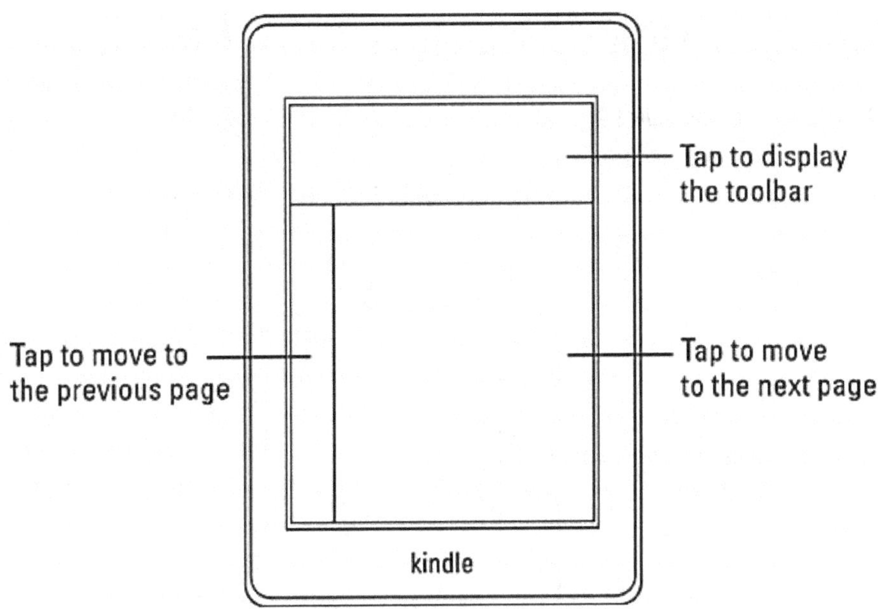

The three zones work as follows:

Top zone When reading a book, a click on the surface shows two toolbars.

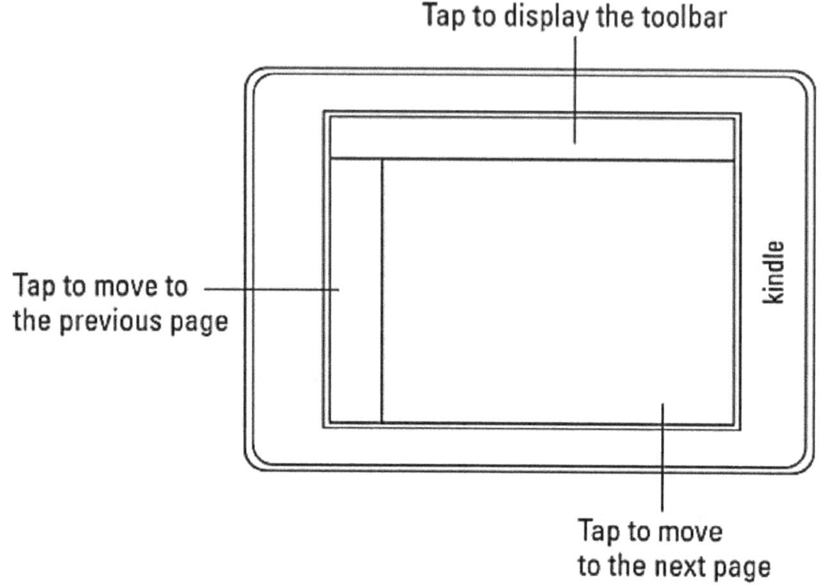

Central Zone: It is largest of the three zones, and covers the center of the screen. Quick tips or millions of your users share here on the next page.

Left area: A crown in the left column goes to the front. Because this area is narrow, your writing should be correct. That said, if you can see the area on the screen, remind me where to write is easier.

CHAPTER FIVE

REMOVE TITLES FROM YOUR SENTENCES

You can remove titles you do not want in your sentences.

To delete titles from your sentences:

- Go to Amazon to see your suggestions.
- Select the View All and Manage link above the suggested titles.
- Click the Remove Articles button at the top of the page.
- Select Remove under the new title.

CHAPTER SIX

HOW TO DELETE BOOKS FROM YOUR KINDLE

Deleting books you no longer want from your Kindle to avoid confusion is easy. Here's everything you need to know

To remove a book from your Kindle device or app, tap the cover of the book you want to delete and select "Delete from device" from the drop-down menu.

HOW TO DELETE A BOOK FROM THE KINDLE LIBRARY

While the above steps remove the book from the Kindle itself, it remains in the Kindle library and you can download it in seconds in the Kindle or Kindle application.

- Open the Amazon website on your smartphone, tablet or computer and sign in (Note that this does not work if you use the Amazon app)

- From the Account menu, click "Content and devices" If it's on your smartphone or "Manage my content and devices" If on a computer

- Check the box next to the books you want to remove from your account.

- On your smartphone, click the three dots next to the check box and select Delete from the menu. On a computer, tap the Delete button at the top of the screen

You will be notified that this will permanently delete the book from the Kindle library. To permanently delete the book. Click "yes,

WHAT ABOUT BOOKS FROM THE KINDLE LOAN LIBRARY

If you have a Kindle and an Amazon Prime subscription, you can borrow one book a month from Amazon's 600,000 powerful library for free, just as you can borrow one book from a public library.

There is no expiration date for the return of the book, but in order to borrow another book, you must return what you have already borrowed.

You can delete the book from your Kindle in the same way you would with any other.

CHAPTER SEVEN

DOWNLOAD COLLECTIONS TO YOUR KINDLE E-READER

Modify your home screen view to display your collections.

From your Kindle home screen, select All to display your content. When your device is set to Home screen view, select your library and then all.

SELECT FILTER AND THEN COLLECTIONS.

- Select the menu icon (three dots) in the gallery you want to download, then select Add to Download. Collected collections display a star symbol.

- Select the collection you want to open, then select a title to open the content or download it to your device.

TO DELETE ITEMS FROM A COLLECTION OR TO DELETE A COLLECTION

Open the collection and click the menu icon. You will see options for adding / removing items, renaming a collection, and deleting a collection. Not all books will be deleted if you delete a collection.

CHAPTER EIGHT

CHILD PROFILE ON YOUR KINDLE E-READER

Set up a child profile to use on Amazon FreeTime.

If you a Kindle on Amazon FreeTime, all you need to do is go to the menu, click on Exist Amazon FreeTime, and imput your parental control PIN to create another child profile.

- In the Home screen click Menu icon,.
- Select Amazon FreeTime.
- Select Add Child Profile.
- Give your parents the PIN code, if necessary, then the name, birthday and gender of the child.
- You can select any content from your own library that you want to include in the child library, then click Next.
- You can also check your child's profile and reading settings, to be everything are in place then select Done.

CHAPTER NINE

ZOOM IN ON IMAGES

You can increase the size of an image in a Kindle book to make it easier to view. Press and hold your own Finger on the image, then release it to display a magnifying glass icon, and then click the Icon. To return the image to its normal size, click on the image again. For selected Kindle books, you can continue zooming by placing two fingers in a row in the center of the screen and move them apart. To zoom out, place two fingers slightly away from the screen and touch them together.

CHAPTER TEN

INTERACT WITH YOUR DOCUMENTS

The Kindle gives you access to features not available with print media such as:

View instant word definitions, easy access to footnotes and book endings.

TO CHANGE YOUR DEFAULT DICTIONARY:

- On the Home screen, move the Menu button and select Settings.
- Open the Settings, and click Device Options, and select Language and Dictionaries.
- Select Dictionaries.
- The currently selected dictionary is displayed under the dictionary language.
- Use the radio button to select the dictionary you want to use, and then click OK.

To check the definition of a word while reading, press and tap to select the word. The box appears with the word definition. If the selected word is also an X-Ray theme, Smart Lookup shows the X-Ray tab. For more information, see the x-ray.

SEARCH

To perform a search, click the search button to display the search box and screen Keyboard. Once you have read, tap at the top of the screen to pick up the toolbars, then click on the Search button and enter the text you are looking for.

If you search from the Home screen, the default title and author search is on mine Items that contain your data in the cloud, as well as those in the Kindle. Your Kindle display active title / author matches in a drop-down menu when entering search criteria. To go directly to an item, click Match in the drop-down menu. If a match is found for a book, then it will last page you are reading.

Press the arrow button to the right of the search bar or the back key on the keyboard to start a complete search. Click on the left side of the search box to display all search filter options:

My items, all the text, the Kindle store, the dictionary and Wikipedia.

If you search while reading, the default search is in the current book / document. Click the left of the search box to display all search filter options that are the same as these on the home screen

To exit the search, type X on the right side of the search bar.

BOOKMARKS

Amazon Whisper sync technology automatically saves you space and content reading. A black bookmark will appear at the top right corner of the page. The Bookmark button on the toolbar changes from white to black on bookmark pages.

You can see a list of all your bookmarks in a book by clicking the Bookmark button in the reading toolbar or by clicking on the top right corner of the page. To bookmark Page or place, type any bookmark in the list. To go to the selected location, press inside Preview. To stay on the current page and turn off bookmarking, tap outside Preview. To delete a bookmark, click the Bookmark button on the Reading Toolbar, look for the bookmarks you like to delete the list, type the bookmark to select it, and then click the X close to it.

Bookmarks are attached to a file on the home screen called My Clippings. When comments the backup is set to On, these things are stored in the cloud for you so they are not lost.

FOOTNOTES

To quickly insert a footnote without going to the end of a book, press the footnote.

Go to the selected footnote position, scroll to the bottom of the footnote and press Go to Footnotes. To return to your home location, press X in the preview window. Remember that not all books supports the footnote.

Books support the possibility of footnotes.

BEFORE YOU GO.

The Before you go... appears when you reach the end of a book or after slippin on the last page of a book. Allows you to rate the book with stars.

CHAPTER ELEVEN

HOW TO LOOK IN A BOOK ON YOUR KINDLE FIRE

Want to find this previous reference to a character so you can stick with a plot? Or do you want to find a reference to Einstein in an online encyclopedia? To find words or phrases in a book on Kindle Fire, you can use the search feature.

This steps will be of help:

- With a book open, tap the page to display the options bar, if needed.
- Click the Search button in the options bar.
- The Search dialog box and on-screen keyboard appear.
- Enter a search term or phrase, and then click the search button on the keyboard.

Search results are displayed.

If you prefer to browse the web, type a word or phrase to highlight it, and then in the resulting dialog box, click the

More button. At this point, you can either type in a book search, search Wikipedia, or do a Google search.

The Google option takes you to the search results for the term in the Google search engine, and the Wikipedia option takes you to the entry in the popular online encyclopedia that matches the search term. Press the Back button when you want to return to the E-Reader application.

CHAPTER TWELVE

VOCABULARY BUILDER

The words you see in the dictionary are automatically added to the Vocabulary Builder. Be seen Word list and quiz yourself with flashcards, type Vocabulary Builder at Home Display or select it from the menu on the Home screen or while reading a book.

To view your glossary, type words at the top left of the screen. Click on a specific word to see it Definition and example of use. To see your words with the book, click on the Books link.

Each time you click Flashcards, Vocabulary Builder selects a set of words from current list and display them as flash cards. To see the definition of a word, click "View Definition" in the upper left corner of the flash card. Click the Learn link on the main page of the Vocabulary Builder Screen to see how many words you are currently learning and how many you already have dominated.

TRUN OFF VOCABULARY BUILDER

To turn off Vocabulary Builder, tap and hold Vocabulary Builder at Home

Screen and select Disable vocabulary creation. You can also turn it off by going to Settings, Reading options and vocabulary creation tool. Remember that the words you are looking for are not included in Vocabulary creation when out. To re-enable the Vocabulary Builder, go to Settings, Reading Options and vocabulary creation tool.

CHAPTER THIRTEEN

KINDLE FREETIME

Kindle FreeTime lets you create a personalized experience for up to four children full control of the content that every child has access to. Children deserve benefits that help monitor their personal readability.

Children can only read books that you have attached to their library.

SET UP THE KINDLE FREETIME

Tap Kindle FreeTime on the Home screen to get started. You are asked to sit down a parental control password if you do not already have one. To create a profile for your child, enter the name, date of birth and gender of your child.

A list of titles will then appear in the Kindle library. Click the check box next to an article title to add it to your child's kindle FreeTime library, click OK.

Set access to benefits On to allow your child to see the benefits. Use the Daily Reading Goal option to specify the number of minutes your child should read Day.

You can create s many profiles as you wish. To customize a profile later, tap the profile icon close to the child's name. Options includes Edit and Delete. The delete option permanently deletes the profile with the reading reading statistics and all the achievements they deserve.

To hide the Kindle FreeTime, tap and hold Kindle FreeTime on the Home screen and tap on Disable Kindle FreeTime. To access or reactivate the Kindle FreeTime, press Menu button and select Kindle FreeTime. To start a session for your child, open the Kindle starts FreeTime and click on your child's name.

KINDLE FREETIME

Press the activity button in the upper left corner to see the number of achievements, progress towards daily reading goal, page reading, reading hours, complete books and total number of words displayed. Use the arrows to see the progress of the last week. Click the date for the achievements of the day, the month and in total. Click the Success link in the upper left corner to see what achievements your child has achieved.

Pressing the progress button displays the same book and the activity link you see and the Achievements link if you have chosen to enable access Performance selection.

CHAPTER FOURTEEN

GOODREADS ON THE KINDLE

Goodreads on Kindle lets you connect with the Goodreads community to see what your friends are reading and share and review books. Click the Goodreads button on the toolbar to start. you will be prompted to sign in to Goodreads or create a new account if you did not do this when creating the Kindle.

When you sign up with an existing Goodreads account, you can see what your friends are reading and see your desire to read, the moment to read and read shelves.

When you create a new account, you have the option to select readers you can follow. If you log in with your Facebook account, all Facebook friends on Goodreads are automatically added to your Goodreads friends list.

You will then be taken to a list of your book purchases on Amazon, digital and physical.

Click the shelf icon to shelve your book.. Remember that rating a book automatically adds it to your reading shelf if it does not exist. Shelve and rated books will become visible to all your friends to see. You can always remove a shelve book later by clicking on the shelf icon and selecting Remove from Shelf. Select Skip to Profile screen and check the shelves, your friends and the latest updates.

There are three tabs in the top corner:

Updates: Check for recent updates. To see a person's profile. Click on their name

My Shelves: Choose to rate a book, update your reading status for a book, add Amazon books.

Friends: See what your friends are reading and find readers to follow. You can also filter by Friends, people who follow you and people who follow you.

There is also a profile icon that you click to view your Goodreads profile.

Goodreads Tips on Kindle:

- Tap the shelf icon to mark a book as read, read or want to read.
- Click on a book to read reviews and see details in the Kindle Store.

- Look for your friends, accept their friend request and see the Goodreads book suggestions at www.goodreads.com.

To use Goodreads on your Kindle, you must have a Wi-Fi connection.

HOW TO SHARE HIGHLIGHTS AND NOTES ON KINDLE PAPERWHITE WITH GOODREADS

When creating or viewing bookmarks and notes in your book, a share button is available on the Kindle Paperwhite This button allows you to share a note and a link to your selected Goodreads transition. If you link your Goodreads account to Facebook and Twitter, your notes will also be shared on this site. You can do all this directly from the Kindle Paperwhite - no computer required!

When you use Kindle Paperwhite to share on Twitter, your tweet consists of your short note and a Goodreads link to a list of excerpts for the book you are reading.

From Kindle Paperwhite you can also update the status of Facebook.

To take advantage of these features, you must connect Kindle Paperwhite to Goodreads. Then add Facebook and Twitter.

To get started, tap the G icon (for Goodreads) on the toolbar.

If you already have a Goodreads account, click Sign in to an existing account. You can use your Facebook account if you are affiliated with Goodreads or just use the Goodreads login as shown in the figure below.

If you do not have an existing account, click Create New Account. The following screen appears and asks you to create a Goodreads account with your Amazon login.

When you create your Goodreads account, you will see screens that allow you to connect with Facebook and Twitter. You can also make these connections later. To connect or make changes to your Facebook account, you need to go to Goodreads on your computer.

This steps will helps:

Press Menu σεις Settings. Reading options Tips for social networks. (If the radio is not turned off, you will be asked to turn it on.)

Click the Connect Account for Twitter button.

Enter your Twitter email address and Twitter password in the authorization screen that appears.

Once the Kindle Paperwhite is connected, you can share a note of what you read with these steps:

- From a book, select text by typing and pressing a word, then slide your finger across the page.
- Click the Share button.
- Enter your message in the text field that appears.
- Click Share

Your note and a link to the selected book snippet in the accounts you linked to Kindle Paperwhite (Goodreads, Twitter, Facebook). All comments are shared on Goodreads. You can share on Twitter and Facebook by clicking and selecting (or deselecting) the box in front of the Twitter and Facebook logos, as shown in the figure below.

You can share Twitter and Facebook updates for magazines and personal documents. Shared items appear on your Facebook wall (as a status update) and are posted from your Twitter account. These comments will be linked to your Kindle.amazon.com page. Comments you share from magazines and personal documents will not be published in Goodreads - Goodreads is for books only

Once you have completed a book, you can rate it and share it on Amazon and Goodreads

CHAPTER FIVETEEN

HOW TO USE THE KINDLE PAPERWHITE BROWSE

The browser is not as complete as the one you are browsing on your computer, but it is an easy-to-use but degraded browser that you can take advantage of if you are out with Kindle Paperwhite somewhere and need to connect quickly.

If you have a Kindle Paperwhite 3G, free 3G internet browsing is limited. You can access the Amazon website and Wikipedia via 3G wireless. You must have a Wi-Fi connection to access other sites.

While the Kindle Paperwhite web browser is simple, it offers some exciting features.

Although Internet access is restricted to 3G Wireless, this access is free. You can access Amazon or Wikipedia anytime, anywhere with your Kindle Paperwhite 3G - as long as you are in an area used by the AT&T mobile network used by Kindle Paperwhite.

The web browser offers a convenient way to connect to the Internet when you are on a Wi-Fi hotspot. This hotspot could be your home without a wired network or Wi-Fi available at a cafe or airport, for example.

For plain text-oriented sites, such as mobile versions of most sites, the easy access to the Internet on your Kindle Paperwhite may be available as a lifesaver - or at least a time saver.

In contrast, the basic nature of the Kindle Paperwhite web browser has a number of disadvantages, including:

The large screen of the Kindle Paperwhite is less than ideal for most Internet users. If you visit sites that are rich in graphics and colors, you will have a less engaging experience.

The web browser does not support sites that use Flash or Shockwave multimedia effects.

Java gadgets are not supported. Some sites use Java gadgets for animation or to provide complex functionality.

Videos cannot be played through the web browser.

The web browser may not be available in some countries outside the US.

HOW TO CONNECT TO THE INTERNET

To access the web browser, click the menu icon on the Home screen, and then click Experimental Browser.

The first time you start your browser, a default list of site bookmarks appears, with Amazon at the top. Tap on one of the bookmarks to open the bookmarks page in your browser

CHAPTER SIXTEEN

SCREENSHOT

Having as many smartphones as we have, we are used to displaying things we love. This is why Amazon also introduced the screenshot feature on their paper. The Kindle Paperwhite is the only Kindle reader with this feature.

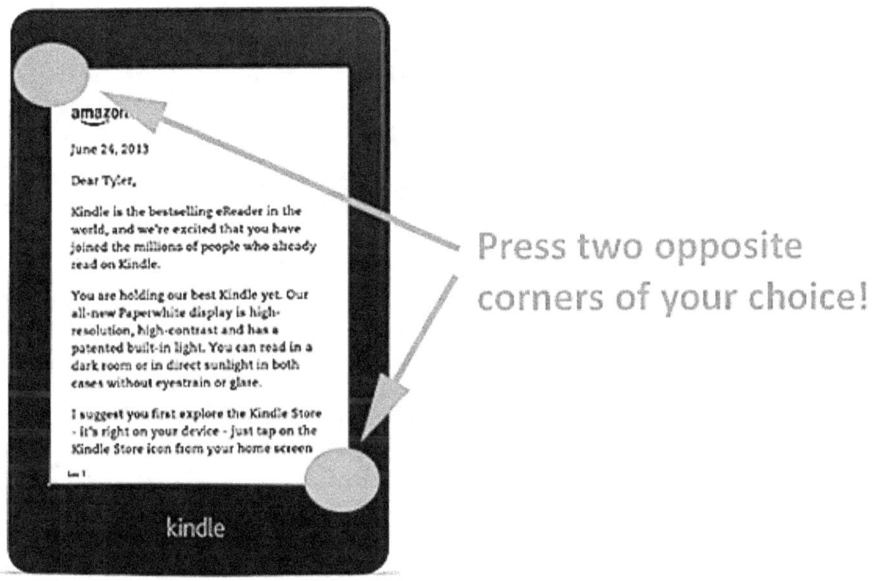

All you have to do to take a screenshot is either the top right corner and the bottom left corner or the top left corner and the bottom left corner of the screen. If you see a flash, you have successfully taken the screenshot. Even if you have to connect the Kindle to your computer to see it.

CHAPTER SEVENTEEN

HOW TO USE THE KINDLE MATCHBOOK

While a few things suggest opening a good book and turning the page, like many old forms of entertainment, do not always make sense in the modern world. The Kindle Matchbook is a program that allows Amazon customers who have purchased physical books to receive a discount on the e-book version of the same title. The price can be from $2.99

It does not work with every book purchase, as only a few publishers and authors have chosen to participate in the program. By the way, Amazon says on its website that there are "thousands of eligible books", so it may only be useful in a few cases

A nice advantage of the matchbook is that it is retro, so if you have been buying books from Amazon since 1999 you may already be eligible for some discounts. It is quite easy to find out if you qualify by searching on the Amazon website. Click on the yellow button labeled "Find Kindle Race Book Titles". You will have to sign in.

Once registered, you will be notified if any of your previous purchases qualify for the Kindle Matchbook. From the same page you can also browse and scroll through all Kindle Matchbook titles and click on more links.

The link will also take you to a page titled Kindle Matchbook and from there you can use the above search to see if the book you want is appropriate

After using the Kindle Matchbook Discount to purchase the eBook Edition, the title will be linked to your Amazon account and accessible from any device where you read Kindle books. The kindle matchbook will help you get more value from your book.

CHAPTER EIGHTEEN

HOW TO BORROW BOOKS ON KINDLE PAPERWHITE

You can borrow an e-book for anyone - even if the person does not have a Kindle Paperwhite! All you need is the person's email address and a book that has been lent.

You can borrow ebooks from your computer. Follow these steps to borrow:

- Open a web browser on your PC and go to your Kindle Manager page.
- If necessary, log in.
- Scroll down to view e-books in the Kindle Library.
- Hold the cursor over the action button for the e-book you want to borrow.
- If an e-book loan has been activated, then a loan comes with this title option.
- Click Pay for this title.
- Enter the email address and name of the person and also a message.

The e-book lender receives an e-mail from Amazon. The loan has seven days to get the loan by clicking on the proof of your loan book now in the email.

What if the person you borrowed the ebook from does not have a Kindle? No problem! You can use many devices to read Kindle ebooks.

The lender can repay the borrowed e-book before the 14-day loan expires. If you read a borrowed book and want to get it back, go to your order section on the Kindle Management page on Amazon. Click the plus sign (+) next to the borrowed title, and then click Delete this title.

Currently, only e-book customers residing in the United States can borrow Kindle e-books. Loans can be made to people living outside the US, but the lender may not accept the loan, depending on geographical differences and publishing rights.

Want to know if a book can be borrowed before you buy it? From your computer or phone, you can view the book's product page in Amazon. Scroll down to Product Details and search for Loans: Enabled. While an e-book is borrowed from your Kindle, you can not read it. You can also borrow a book only once.

CHAPTER NINETEEN

HOW TO READ EPUB ON KINDLE PAPERWHITE

Is EPUB compatible with Kindle? To get started, let's wait a few minutes for the answer to this question. After transferring ebook files in epub format to Kindwhite, we can not see any of them from the home page. These transferred files are not listed. Why couldn't we find and open the epub directly on kindle paperwhite? This is because:

- Kindle Paperwhite only supports users who purchase books from the Kindle Store. And these books are in their exclusive Kindle eBook format, like kfx, mobi, etc. Because epub is not an ebook format supported by Kindle, it cannot be found on Kindle devices, although it has been ported to Kindle.

- Most of the Epub books we bought, such as Google Ebooks, Kobo, Sony, are DRM protected, which prevents us from reading Epub files to unsupported readers, such as the Kindle paperwhite.

Once you find the reasons, the solutions will be easily found. The first thing to do is:

CONVERT EPUB TO KINDLE FORMAT (3 WAYS)

Reading ePub on Kindle Paperwhite is the best and easiest way to convert files. As we all know that Kindle reads Kindle format, what about converting Epub format to Kindle Readable?

How can I convert epub to Kindle ebook format? Kindle ebook Converter is the tool you need. I present 3 effective tools.

TOOL 1: CONVERT EPUB TO CALIBER

As an ebook fan, have you heard of Caliber? This is a free ebook management tool that helps you convert ebooks from one format to another. So you can use it to convert epub files to candle format.

Download Caliber and get started. You can now add the downloaded Epub books, and select them then tap the Convert Books icon.

adds epub to caliber

From the pop-up window, select "Mobi" as your hydrogen form. The best file format supported by Kindle is Mobi. Then click "OK".

converts epub to Kindle Mobi with caliber

Price: Free

Good point: Convert any form to another. edit metub metadata? read epub around the computer as a reader.

Weakness: You need to install the DRM Removal plugin to convert drmed epub files.

bad caliber point

TOOL 2: CONVERT EPUB TO ACTIVATION WITH ONLINE CONVERTER

Having trouble installing third-party software? An online converter is a good choice. Easily convert Epub books to Kindle via the web.

Epubor - Support various forms of conversion, epub output, pdf and mobi.

Zamzar - Famous for free file conversion on the internet, and also writes a few words to suggest file extension.

CloudConvert - 199 formats supported, and also introduces file extension. It can also help you upload a file to Dropbox.

Price: Free

Good point: You do not need to install on the computer. Convert files very quickly.

CHAPTER TWENTY

KINDLE DICTIONARY GUIDE:

HOW TO ADD, EDIT, AND CREATE PERSONALIZED KINDLE DICTIONARIES

Most people have misinformation about how dictionaries work in Kindle ebook readers, so I wanted to write this guide and explain how to edit, add, and create dictionaries for Kindle devices.

Last week, someone left a comment and complained about how candles suck compared to Kobos because kids do not allow you to use your own dictionaries. I knew this was not right, because it's easy to upload dictionaries to the Kindles, as long as they are in the correct format.

In addition, the Kindle is pre-installed with some English dictionaries, along with a bundle of free foreign language dictionaries that you can download from the cloud.

There are also many free Kindle dictionaries in MOBI format that you can download online.

If you do not find the dictionary you are looking for on the Internet or in the Kindle Store, you can even create your own Kindle dictionaries from dictionary databases whenever you want.

HOW TO CHANGE THE DEFAULT KINDLE DICTIONARY

- Go to Settings> Device Options> Language & Dictionaries> Dictionaries to select from the downloaded dictionaries (you can add more to display here, see sections below).

You can also quickly change dictionaries while reading by selecting a word, and then clicking the dictionary name in the lower-right corner of the window.

Including foreign language dictionaries

Most people are not aware that their Kindle comes with many language dictionaries, at least one for every language it supports.

Additionally, you can find all the dictionaries on your Content and Device Management page on Amazon. Select to display dictionaries and user guides.

The current composition of the Kindles is accompanied by the following free foreign language dictionaries:

- Spanish
- Chinese
- Russian
- Dutch
- Japanese
- German
- Italian
- French language
- Portuguese

There is more that you can get at the Kindle Store.

HOW TO CREATE CUSTOM KINDLE DICTIONARIES

Here is a step-by-step guide to creating your own Kindle dictionaries for free. The process works in any language.

Fantasy dictionaries

Some have taken custom dictionaries to a whole new level. The novels take advantage of Kindle's built-in dictionary function to provide additional details about specific books. They contain terms and content specifically for the book you are reading. It's like a more advanced version of the Kindle X-Ray feature.

There are fiction for popular fantasy and science fiction epics, such as George Song's A Song of Ice and Fire and Robert Jordan's Wheel of Time. There are fiction for classic writing by Mark Twain and Jane Austen.

Check the Fictionary website for more information and free downloads.

CHAPTER TWENTY ONE

CUSTOMIZE YOUR TEXT DISPLAY

Your Kindle offers a quick way to customize the appearance of books and magazines. A dialog box appears asking you to change the font size, line space and content margins on the Kindle screen. The editor's font option is available on selected books that include the ability to view publisher embedded fonts.

You may be asked to update your Kindle when new fonts are available.

COMIC AND MANGA BOOK

Comics and manga come to life with Kindle's dashboard view. To access the Kindle dashboard view, double click on the screen. To navigate through the panels, press your finger on the screen or touch the sides of the screen. To exit Kindle Dashboard view, double-tap the screen again.

CHILDREN'S BOOKS

Some Kindle children's books have Kindle Text pop-ups for reading text over pictures. You can Navigate between pop-up sections of text by swiping your hand on the screen or touch the sides of the screen. Selected children's books are automatically opened in this view. To disable the text appears and returns to normal reading, tap on the screen twice.

CHAPTER TWENTY TWO

MANAGE YOUR KINDLE LIBRARY

Your Kindle Paperwhite can store over a thousand books, personal documents, newspapers, blogs, magazines, and active content collectively named "Contents" in this guide. To display a list of content on your Kindle Paperwhite, touch the start button. To see how much free space you have to store content, from the home screen, click the Menu button and click Settings. On the Settings page, tap the menu button and select Device Information.

You can view the content of the home screen using the standard or traditional list view.

To change the appearance of the home screen, touch the Menu button and select List or Cover view.

To filter your content by type, on the home screen, touch My items below the toolbar.

Filter options include all articles, books, periodicals, documents, collections, and active content.

To jump to a specific title or page, go to the home screen and click the page number control.

For example, 1/2 indicates that you are on page 1 and you have 2 pages of content on your Kindle.

When the dialog box is displayed, enter the page number you want to go to or the first letter of the page or the author name(depending on your current sorting option).

WITH COLLECTIONS

Your collections are in sync in the middle of other devices and applications that are connected to the same Amazon account and are compatible with collections in the cloud. Items can also be added to more than collection. Please note that newspapers, magazines and blogs can not be added currently to collections. For information on devices and applications that support cloud collections, **visit www.kindle.com/support.**

TO CREATE A NEW COLLECTION

- Tap the Menu button.
- Choose to create a new collection.

- Use the keyboard to type a name for the collection, and then click OK. A list of items on your Kindle that can be displayed in a collection. Remember that magazines and blogs cannot be added in collections.
- 4. Touch the check box next to an item to add it to the collection, then click Done when finished.

You can add or remove items at a later time by clicking the menu button when in collection and select Add or Remove Items.. To exit a collection, touch the Home button.

To filter the content on your home screen by collection, touch My Items and select Collections.

To set a collection to appear in all views, touch and hold a collection's cover or collection title, and then click Show in all views. Please note that these settings are device specific. To change this setting, press and hold the cap of the collection or title, and then click show only and collections view.

TIPS ON CLOUD COLLECTIONS

- If you have existing collections from older devices or other reading applications, they automatically import the first time you register a device or application to read that supports cloud collections.

- Delete a collection created on a device or in a cloud-enabled reading app collections, like your Kindle Paperwhite, delete them from the cloud and other devices or read applications that support collections in the cloud and are registered in the same Amazon account.

- Delete a collection imported by unsupported device or reader collections in the cloud will not affect the original collection on other reading devices or applications.

- Deleting a collection from your Kindle does not delete the content stored on your device or in the clouds. Items previously added to the collection stored on your Kindle appear on the home screen after deleting the collection.

- When you unsubscribe from your Kindle, the Cloud Collection settings will not be saved.

www.ingramcontent.com/pod-product-compliance
Lightning Source LLC
Chambersburg PA
CBHW071948120726

48001CB00005B/2093